Christmas, 1999

NORTH WOODS WALKABOUT

A Maine Odyssey

Nan Turner Waldron

Butterfly & Wheel Publishing
*A blending of the natural world and a
creative philosophy of life*

1998

Illustrations by Vera Cross, Sharon, Massachusetts.

Photographs by the author. Back cover photograph by Toby
Montgomery. Cover design by Design Point, Epping, NH.

Produced by: J. N. Townsend Publishing, Exeter, New
Hampshire.

Printed in the United States.

Also by the Author
Journey to Outermost House

Published by
Butterfly & Wheel Publishing
145 Flanders Road
Bethlehem, CT 06751

ISBN: 0-9630546-1-9

Library of Congress Cataloging-in-Publication Data
Waldron, Nan Turner.
North woods walkabout / Nan Turner Waldron.
p.   cm.
Includes bibliographical references.
1. Waldron, Nan Turner. 2. Piscataquis County (Me.)--Description and travel. 3. Maine--Description and travel. 4. Natural
history--Maine. 5. Spiritual biography--Maine. I. Title.
f27.P5W35   1998   98-47517
917.41--dc21   CIP

To my mother
who died young but whose laughter and
lovely face I easily recall.

To my father
who died before I could thank him for his
patience, love and support.

Their spirits touch me still.

"I have always been fond of linnaea (twinflower) because it grows in the shadows, away from the direct glare of the sun, seems a part of big time and the depths of the wilderness ... shy and delicate, would shrivel to nothing if protection were gone or the rains did not come in time. As fragile as solitude, they would disappear at the slightest intrusion."

Sigurd F. Olson, *Wilderness Days*

PROLOGUE

"Though the country has changed since the mid-nineteenth century, its character remains the same for you as it did for Thoreau. It is still a frontier for the mind, heart and spirit."
—J. Parker Huber writing about the Maine woods, *The Wildest Country*

Over the years I have read a great deal about songlines, walkabouts and the deeper level of a vision quest, but never felt that these experiences applied to me, and certainly never thought of myself as being on any kind of quest. Questing brings to mind the wandering of ancient tribes or mystics, neither of which seemed remotely connected to me as a wife, mother and grandmother. Then one day at a yard sale I found an old leather-bound book titled *Indians of the United States*, written in 1882 by Clark Wissler who, while serving as an army officer, had made a detailed study of the traditions, customs and theology of our western Indians. He noted, "When he (the Indian) seeks wisdom and light, he goes out alone and, deep in the presence of nature, opens his mind and heart." This description struck a chord within me. I knew immediately that this sort of experience was very much like my own—although wisdom was a long way from my mind whenever I set out on a short walk, or a day's hike, or a canoe trip. But now that I am older and have the advantage of perspective I realize that I have indeed been on a quest because questing is what we humans are all about. Whether we are at home or abroad in the world, whether we are alone or with a companion, unknown or famous, we are ever in search of the essence of being. We are born trying to understand self, seeking a core of truth, pondering the unknown, all the time hoping to recognize a connection with some profound purpose beyond our brief existence.

While wandering in the north woods of Maine I have been and still am on a quest. Others may begin their quest through yoga, religious studies, meditation, reading or any kind of solitary confrontation which inspires creative understanding. I have simply returned to a pattern begun during childhood summers in Maine where the northwoods always seemed to speak to me. As I look back upon my life's journey it is fascinating to discover the delicate influences which taught me to be at home in the natural world.

A SENSE of BELONGING

"But the things I remember best are clouds in the sky, stars in the heavens and the fragrance of the forest as I walked in the wood roads."—James Kavanugh, *Weary of Wrestling*

Forest trails and narrow wood roads have been familiar to me since childhood when my father, before he left for his law office in Boston, took us on early morning excursions through the Middlesex Fells near our home in Malden, Massachusetts, and in later years on hikes in New Hampshire and Maine. We four children would follow behind him wearing snowshoes or "India" rubber boots as we laughingly called them (Father often read to us and one favorite was *The Peterkin Papers* in which the little boys always wore their "India" rubber boots) or whatever the weather required, discovering all manner of wonderful things. In spring we carried jars to hold pond water astir with insect life; in winter when he sometimes pulled us on a toboggan we found snow fleas and mammal tracks and ice-covered waterfalls.

Once he called in a great-horned owl whose big eyes stared down at us from so close we didn't have to take turns looking through his WWI army issue binoculars to see it. Father did not shoot a bird in order to identify it as was still the custom among ornithologists of his day. Although he did insist that each of us learn to handle a gun as a matter of safety, he never shot anything. In fact he even treated wild plants with the utmost care, digging up and carrying unfamiliar specimens in a moistened cloth sugar bag tied to his belt and carefully returning them after he had keyed them out at home. In those days there were no practical field guides to refer to, no small cameras with macro lenses to capture a flower, no telephoto lenses to record a bird sighting or for that matter no widespread interest in their migratory habits except among hunters or professional biologists. For the general public all of that was 30 years in the future. The 1926 printing of Frank Chapman's book *Birdlife* featured colored plates and urged teachers to emphasize the habits of birds rather than the structural classification so that the public might begin to enjoy what they were seeing. My father was way ahead of that! A copy of the beautiful plates which accompanied Forbush's *Birds of Massachusetts* lay open on a table in front of the window where we fed the winter birds. *Enjoy* is exactly what our exposure to the outdoor world was all about. Beyond the walls of our little home nature performed in an endless pageant akin to our own living and being.

When my brother was five and we girls were eight, nine and eleven years old our parents took us to Maine for our first real vacation away from home—and not just "any old place" in Maine either. Oh no. Maine is a huge state, the size of Connecticut, Massachusetts, New Hampshire and Vermont combined, and has a wide variety of terrain. We were heading 300 miles north of Boston to Greenville, which in 1930 was a long, slow two-day trip by car.

Bill Caldwell wrote in his book *Enjoying Maine*, "The north country is a world wholly different from the rest of Maine." And that is where we went, to the north country, to Greenville, a logging/mill town a long way from anywhere, "the end of the road" with a hundred miles of woods beyond. Even in 1982 an article in *Yankee Magazine* read, "Greenville still looks like an outpost town." The village and the junction where the trains used to arrive border the southern shore of Moosehead Lake, the largest lake in New England and the Squaw Mountains form a long protective wall on the west side of town. On summer evenings the sunsets crown the mountain peaks with clouds of flaming colors creating a broad panarama of shining water and shadowy blue ridges outlined against a blazing sky—a scene poised to speak to the spirit.

This was the gateway to the Allagash, the great river of the north, Thoreau's country, the last great wilderness. Not any more, to be sure, but it has remained forever wild to me. And this land which became beloved by us all would be our summer home away from home for many years to come.

On this first visit we children had no way of knowing that the Walden Farm northeast of Greenville where we would be staying had been chosen for a particular reason and that this would be our only vacation together as a complete family. Our parents, faced with the painful reality that my mother was dying of cancer, were laying plans for the future. Nothing was ever said about her illness, at least not to my knowledge and we children were too young to ask the right questions. Her death the next year came as a puzzling shock to me. My grandmother with whom I was staying the nights said to me one morning, using words I had never heard before, "Your mother has passed away." So I ran home to find out if we were passing with her. Father was more straightforward: he called it death but indeed it was a passing for us all into subtly new patterns. There was no mourning, no words of woe and no lament for the burdens now on my father's mind. He said just one thing, "Never be bitter about death. It is part of living." And I have been eternally grateful to him for his choice of words. But that was all he said so I have no image of my mother, his beloved wife. There were no diaries or letters to read, no stories to hear from aged relatives which could have created a picture of my parents as a couple.

My father was not the type to discuss his personal life with anyone, especially his children. Temperamentally, he and I were miles apart. I am emotional and outspoken, not apt to suffer in silence. He, fortunately for us children, was a quiet man blessed with infinite patience. I never heard him complain but I wish now that he had been more talkative. There were only a few times when he allowed me even a brief glimpse of his own memories with which to enhance my impressions of the past. One such opening came when I was sixteen. He and I were going to Greenville for the 30th of May weekend. We joked about riding alone anywhere with father. "Who did you talk with?" He took it kindly. So, as usual, he drove with a cigar in his mouth and I relaxed in the familiar silence watching the scenery go by. The air was warming and the fields were turning green. The memory of a long ago field drifted into my mind. I asked, "Do you remember taking us as little kids to a big field where you made us daisy chains and crowns of flowers?"

"Yes," he said quietly, hesitated then continued, "That was practice for me. I took you to a field near home where there were flowers and a brook. When we came home your mother and I talked. She would suggest things I might have done to make the day go more smoothly."

That was all. I was stunned. No comment was possible. My mind pictured a handsome young father sitting in a field braiding daisies for his children, learning to be a mother.

I never see daisies smiling up at the sun but what I think of him.

TAKING THE FAMILY to northern Maine where they had spent their honeymoon was a plan my parents had made together so that my father might have a suitable place to take us on his yearly vacation. Friends had recommended a farm on the outskirts of Greenville which took in guests and was well known for its hospitality. This was Walden Farm, owned by a college-educated couple who had the courage and the resourcefulness to survive the depression on a farm and, more importantly for us, had five children our own ages. I shall never forget the moment when we first drove up in front of the big white farmhouse. As the adults greeted each other we four sat silently in the car sizing-up the five on the porch showing off for our benefit by swinging from the porch beams and balancing on the railings—a hint of challenge to the strangers not yet friends.

Everything about the farm was new. It was a totally different way of life and each day offered another adventure: drinking foamy milk fresh from the cows; the itchy fun of jumping in the hay; gathering warm eggs from under the chickens; pouring slop into a trough over the heads of squealing pigs; using the two-holer in the shed where the old Sears catalogue served as t.p.; climbing spooky back stairs to the unfinished third floor. And everything had fragrance: hot bread and ginger cookies; moist wood beams of the attic;

Beloved Walden Farm. memories and the beautiful views remain. The land and all the big buildings were taken by the government in 1940 to construct an emergency landing site for transports. It is now the town-owned Greenvile Airport.

steamy manure and dusty dry hay; caraway seeds, sweet pea blossoms and rich earth. Oh, it was wonderful and my curiosity danced like a Fourth of July sparkler. There was so much to learn and, except for the big work horses, few things I shied away from.

One day we children were told in no uncertain terms to *stay out of the barn!*

"Why?" I thought."What's the problem in the barn?"

Answers, I wanted answers and I set out to find some. Like any northern farmstead all the buildings were joined for easy passage in winter weather so, to avoid detection, I came down the back stairs into the laundry room beyond the kitchen, went into the shed and through the door to the barn where I hid under the haywagon and waited. Mr. Walden and another man led the calf, the one we had been petting and feeding, into the far end and closed the big door. They tied the calf, killed and dressed it out. I don't think they ever saw me but I spoiled that soon enough. At supper that evening when liver and bacon was served I volunteered the information I had gathered. "I know where this liver came from! Mr. Walden hit the calf with ..." I was going to say "the flat end of the ax" but I couldn't finish. The adults reacted immediately by dismissing me from the table. "That will be enough, Nanny!"

Overreacted I thought. Heck, folks told fishing and hunting stories, mine just happened to be current affairs. Such problems are avoided nowadays. A package of frozen liver garnished with parsley doesn't look much like a cute calf. Most suburban shoppers are so far from the sources of their food that they no longer grasp the reality of the harvest. On the farm I eventually learned to kill chickens for Sunday dinner and to be thankful for the meal. And I learned to fish and to catch, whop, skin and serve frog's legs, a delicacy people now pay good money for now that I would have been happy to supply free of charge. And I learned too, how hard some families had to work, and to admire the grace and joy some people bring to the art of living.

EVERY AUGUST FIRST, after my mother died, my father would load, heap, pack us into his car and head for Greenville. Our mode of transportation was a brown seven-passenger Lincoln touring car the size and efficiency of a Mack truck, a car considered by my stalwart and studious father to be SAFE! It was close to the biggest thing on the road, highways and 16-wheelers being many years into the future. This was 1931 and when we went anywhere we were, to say the least, noticeable! My father, wearing a visored cap, gray wool shirt, knickers, L.L.Bean mocassins and an unlit cigar in his mouth, sat bolt upright behind the great steering wheel. On the running board confined by a foot-high expansion gate were two canvas army buckets full of water. The radiator commonly boiled over on the hills and the buckets had to be refilled at streams along the road. On the long trip north we played number and alphabet games which father was especially good at, "I'm thinking of something red/orange, etc., bird-beast-fish," recited every Burma Shave poem and became generally fidgety as the hours dragged on. There was a huge sign at the edge of the woods a few miles before we reached Greenville. We vied to be the first to see it:

This is GODS country
Why set it on fire
and
Make it look
like HELL!

God's country, where the lakes are cool and the air smells of spruce and balsam and new mown hay. We made it! Just a few minutes more and we would arrive. Our car, laden with luggage, bearskin rugs (really lead-weight wool), driver and four passengers—one in front, three in back dressed in brown suede jackets and red berets—would finally chug down the hill into town at a top speed of 25 miles per hour. Lumbering down the road we must have looked like a huge log with four red-topped British soldier lichen growing on the bark.

YEAR AFTER YEAR we rolled into town, turned right at Sander's store and headed for the farm three miles east on the top of a hill. When the car stopped in front of the big white farmhouse we tumbled out to join our "summer family" letting the familiar emotional warmth of the farm embrace us. There were the cows and horses and golden hay in the barn; there was milk for the calf, scraps for the chickens and slop for the pigs. All as it should be. There was a trout in the deep well (to eat the insects—every "proper farm well" had a trout) and cold wet sawdust in the ice house. The kitchen, with a venerable wood stove, smelled of bacon rind and fresh bread and cookies, and no one sampled the wares unless hands and face were as scrubbed as the wooden floor! Oh, we had such great times together, the Turners and the Waldens! We helped them with chores when we could and they joined us on my father's many excursions.

From the beginning I thought this home was paradise. My young brother did too. I never asked my sisters. They had different goals. What would they know about paradise when they never went barefoot in the pigpen, and they wore cotton gloves to squeeze nightcrawlers onto fish hooks and were much too proper to get involved with frogs' legs and chickens. I liked getting up at dawn to watch the deer in the cool morning mists, to hang around in the barn while the cows were being milked and then wait by the kitchen stove for a fresh doughnut. The day's work began early and was dictated by the demands of farm living, but we were young and knew nothing about the real burdens of this life. We roamed pastures and picked blueberries; we hiked mountains and explored lake shores; we went on picnics and camped overnight. And we sang songs and laughed and filled the empty places in our hearts.

"The lane from Walden Farm winds prettily through field and forest down to the water's edge, where cars may be parked and boats rented. One can scarcely imagine a finer piece of unspoiled wilderness. There is nothing neatly trimmed, and rough timbers and stumps are in clear view, yet there is a pervasive overtone of wild beauty, and the invitation of waiting boats is almost irresistible, since unseen sections of the lake promise more beauty round the points."
—Marion J. Bradshaw, The Maine Land, 1941

TREASURES of the HEART

"It is these small events that make up the legends of our lives."—
Carl A. Hammerschlag, *The Dancing Healers*

Recently, long after I had prepared this part of my own story, I came across a fascinating comment in a collection of Walt Whitman's memoranda in which he mentions scenes from youth and manhood: "... a dream, a picture that for years at intervals has come noiselessly up before me, and I really believe, fiction as it is, has entered largely into my practical life. Sometimes I wake at night and can hear and see it plainly." His words delighted me. I have had the same kind of experience. It is such fun to discover a common bond with another person whether one from my own era or one from long ago. Actually such an unexpected feeling of mutual accord, particularly with someone of years past, brings me closer to understanding Joseph Campbell's thoughts about "a well of universal truths." Thinking alike isn't copying, it is sharing similiar insights and experiences, it is validation, it is "YES! I know what you are saying." If we are willing to listen to our inner selves it becomes obvious that incidents in each of our lives push us in one direction or another with a gentle or jarring thrust. Some we understand immediately, others sift gradually into our awareness, opening doors, allowing change to be an adventure in life.

MY FATHER WAS, naturally, the dominant figure in my early years. He shopped for clothing, sewed on buttons (in those days everything had either buttons or elastic) cut hair, read stories, baked bread, created paper cut-outs, attended to all manner of injuries and complaints and brought an amazing variety of interests to the job of single-parenting. He accepted life as it came and we children did the same. His influence on my life was easy to understand. Another was a surprise. One day as I was leisurely scanning old memories (inner questing I call it) I discovered how much our sojourns in Maine had influenced the shape of my life. The connection was suddenly, delightfully obvious. There, among my early memories, were two scenes which seemed to have been more carefully stored than others. They stood out from the rest: the blueberry fields and the road to the pond. Two beloved recordings still playing.

The Fields:

August was primetime for harvesting the lowbush blueberries for which the Walden Farm was famous. Their berries were shipped by train to Maine's finest hotels. Rowena (we called her Lamb), one of the Walden girls, handled the business so my sisters and I were often out in the field helping. The berries were hand picked, not raked. Never even saw a rake until years later on the coastal blueberry barrens where I watched workers using rakes. It struck me as a destructive way to harvest a good crop, an angry way. I'm glad the Waldens didn't use them. I would never have learned to respect the gifts of the earth if I had been tearing the leaves and the unripe fruit from the plants. When I picked I felt joyful—still do. But it wasn't the picking I remembered so clearly, it was what I thought about while I was "supposed" to be picking. Put me in an open space and I become a mental nomad—ask anyone who has ever gone adventuring with me—I am a daydreamer following after fantasies soon forgotten. Only I hadn't forgotten this one. It had stayed in my mind, reappearing again and again as if it had been trying to get my attention, and evidently had.

I remembered how I would stand in the summer sun gazing west at the blue-green mountains in the distance imagining that I was the forest fire ranger who lived in a snug cabin near the top of Squaw Mountain. Surrounded by the natural world I pictured myself hauling water from a nearby brook, cutting wood for a little stove and when hikers passed by on the trail I would tell them about the plants and wildlife of the forest.

MY LIFE HAS been lived a long way from any mountaintop and I had regarded this fantasy as a sentimental memory from childhood until I discovered the connection. What have I been doing for the past twenty-five years? Living in little remote cabins, hauling water, stoking woodstoves and lecturing people all over New England about the simple wonders of the natural world. My fantasy matched perfectly our cabin in Maine where I stayed summers with the children; those of you who have read my Cape Cod book will recognize more similarities; and anyone who has heard me speak about my wanderings in northern Maine will wonder if I have ever lived anywhere other than in my mountain fantasy. Deep within me there certainly had been a viable seed from that daydream waiting for the proper time to push up through the busy years of my life to find fulfillment. And now I see other ways in which my habit of imaging had carried over into my later years. When I roamed with my children and we stopped to rest I would tell them stories about the "little people" of the forest. Later as their school schedules left me with some free time I led walks at various santuaries in the area introducing others to the birds and plants and the aura of a woodland setting. Then, as an enthusiastic photographer, I began to lecture to the public about the things I had seen or heard and what these experiences have meant to me. The more I shared with others the more aware I became of how much I had learned about myself when I responded to the natural world.

The Road:

There was a road leading from the farm to the pond two miles away which became so familiar that even now I can recall every turn and pitch down to the old log culvert where it crossed the brook and ended on the gravelly shore. The road took us past the broad blueberry fields, over the hilltop with a glorious view to the east of the mountains and ponds, alongside the small orchard where gnarled old apple trees bore sour green fruit (only city kids—I did not consider myself one of course—got sick from eating green apples: sissies who didn't wear high sneakers or carry a hunting knife on the hip), on down into the deep shade of the maple grove to the spruce-lined shore. Whoever got to the empty boathouse first could change to their swimsuits, losers waited. So we kids would run barefoot pell-mell on a shortcut along the brook, cold mud squeezing up between our toes, shouting and racing to the finish. The boys usually won. I can hear our young voices as we laughed our way into the swim; I can feel the soft water smoothing its way over young skin—so cool in the summer sun, so warm in a gray rain. These were the special interludes of summer spanning the enchanted explorations of childhood and the contentious confrontations of youth. A few hours in a lifetime gathering memories to return to. Gifts from the wonders of earth and sky and caring friends and family to share with my own children on new roads in a changing world.

It is not surprising that wood roads entice me. Any kind: abandoned bolder-strewn ones with exposed ledges and rotting log bridges built long ago by lumbermen; rutted roads winding through deserted fields edged by stone walls overgrown by scrubby brush hiding their back breaking history. Wherever I see one I think, "Sometime I will come back to follow that road," as if it were asking me to return to hear its story. Roads look as if they had a story, they're the icon for the story of a journey, one I can follow, as I do my own, finding joy along the way in simple discoveries.

Nowadays simplicity is seldom associated with pleasure. There are those who are mad for newness, eager to see exciting and impressive sights, wild to experience challenges which will be impossibly gratifying. I have friends who urge me to hike high mountain meadows or visit a tropical isle. But I have never longed to travel. The wonders of the world in faraway places do not tempt me. I like to get to know a place, to soak up its atmosphere until I wear it like a pair of old sneakers and a floppy hat. I don't mean to imply that I have become an authority on any aspect of the places which are familiar to me—far from it. Rather, when I feel that I belong to a wild place, it is the place which teaches me about myself, which urges me to open doors, to hear new voices, to review the lessons from earth begun in my childhood. Richard Nelson, writer of the Northwest, comments on the Koyukon peoples' extraordinary relationship with their natural community, which has emerged through carefully observing the same events repeated endlessly over lifetimes and generations. "There may be more to learn," he wrote in *The Island Within*, "by climbing the same mountain a hundred times than by climbing a hundred different mountains." Perceiving wholeness takes much time and neither the natural world nor a human should be assessed from a piecemeal point of view. That would be like abhoring the caterpillar and later admiring the butterfly. As for me, I am not yet a "whole life" either. I must still return to familiar ground, to roots inner and outer, climbing my mountain a hundred times to seek that wholeness which is open ended and flowing with the life force.

LESSONS from FAMILIAR PLACES

"The seat of the soul is there, where the outer and inner worlds meet." —Novalis, 18th century novelist, from *The Inner Reaches of Outer Space* by Joseph Campbell.

A garden is a special place where living things are watched and tended and, while working the soil, many gardeners develop a profound acquaintance with earth. *In Voices from the Earth*, William Longgood states, "... beginnings and endings and the great cycle that welds everything together in an interlocking, interdependent, and indivisible world. It all begins in the soil." My husband raises all sorts of vegetables and flowers. It is work he enjoys. We eat like kings and he has the pleasure of sharing with friends the various fruits of his labor. But I haven't the patience required of gardeners so I cook, can or freeze the produce. Other than that I am of little help. My favorite gardens are woodlands

and bogs where things come up by themselves and I can just ·
walk around and enjoy them. I prefer to go where plants *live*.
Where each belongs to a specific community which belongs
to a wider community of earth which is ultimately tied to the
solar community. I want to be a part of that, to feel how
every cycle entwines with every other cycle. And when I am
in the woods or out on a bog I can recognize these myriad
connections and sense that somehow I too belong to all of it.
Natalie Goldberg writes in *Long Quiet Highway*, "Everything
has its time and is nourished and fed with the rhythms of the
sun and moon, the seasons. We are no different, no more
special, no less important. We belong on the earth. We grow
in the same way as a rock, a snail, a porpoise, or a blade of
grass." I rather think most people are uneasy with this thought
but it makes me feel good. I have always cherished the feeling that I belonged to earth but I had no idea how that would
influence the way in which I would live my life. Earth and I
began long ago with a nodding acquaintance which devel-
oped gradually into a friendly sort of guru-to-student relationship. For as long as I can remember I have considered
earth my instructor. I was quite clearly being guided through
levels of awareness learning only when I was prepared to listen, hearing only what I was ready to understand. When I
look back I can see some of the steps which encouraged me

to open doors and explore new connections and I think it all began because my father had nurtured my sense of wonder.

TALK OF WONDER brings to my mind a marvelous assortment of connections from childhood. Everything from fireflies, meteor showers, waterfalls and thunderstorms to explorers, opera singers and a preacher. The exciting living earth and its inhabitants all filed away in my memories under "wide-eyed wonders." Some were voiceless faces from silent films; some were faceless voices like Lily Pons whose arias through the magic of radio filled our livingroom on a Saturday afternoon; others strode on stage in full costume telling stories of high adventure in far-off places; and one I only heard about when our scholarly Universalist preacher dressed in a billowing black robe rose in the pulpit and told of Jesus walking on the water. It was clear to me that Jesus was right up there with the best of them. And in my mind they all belonged together: the gifts of humans and the mysteries of earth.

NOTHING IN CHILDHOOD presented a moment more thrilling to me than the pageants in the night sky. These days the sky's dramatic events are overwhelmed by city lights , no longer available to lift our spirits. Wouldn't it be wonderful if our communities had regularly scheduled "LIGHTS OUT" celebrations when we would all go outdoors to rediscover that earth is really adrift in the heavens and that the moon and the stars can claim a certain kinship with us. I remember one magical night in Maine when I was about twelve years old. Around midnight my father woke us up, told us to dress warmly, to bring a flashlight and join him on the farmhouse porch because the northern lights were putting on an unusual display. Giving each of us a blanket to carry he led us out across the pasture to the top of the hill overlooking the pond. The sky had a strange glow and above the mountains to the north great shafts of green color pulsed up and down like organ pipes moving to their own rhythm. After a few minutes vaporous clouds of rose and white exploded in the sky overhead. We lay down on our blankets to watch. Suddenly, the center of the heavens was covered with soft rainbows as if someone were shaking a fistful of colored ribbons back and forth across the field of stars. The top of the world had gone wild with decorations! How long did it last? I could not say —perhaps forever. Yes, forever. That is the gift of wonder, it lingers in the spirit like a favorite melody sometimes bringing tearful memories, sometimes joy.

IN THE NORTH WOODS country in early May the flooding streams are crisply cold and the cedar bogs are chilled by pockets of ice still hidden in crevices beneath a carpet of sphagnum moss. The hardwood trees stand bare and exposed on a forest floor pressed flat by the weight of the winter's snow. They wait in eerie silence for the first warm days of spring. Once—it seems years ago, I must have been all of forty—in the early hours of a cool May morning I walked into the woods to a place where I knew the clintonia and lady's-slipper grew. Leaning against a chilly tree trunk I joined the waiting. Slowly, as the sun rose higher, an air of expectation infused me. I could feel a force stirring in the forest surrounding me, as if somehow I were a part of it! Emerson had written, "Nature is made to conspire with spirit to emancipate us." Exactly! I lay down, put one ear to the ground and listened. Faint rustlings! Plugged-in, that's how I felt, plugged-in! I wanted to jump up, run home and tell everyone: "Hey guys! Guess What! I just heard the flowers growing!" Fortunately for my long suffering family I was a long way from home. My mind prodded me to be alert,"There's a message, don't miss the message." I was talking to myself. "Don't get so excited! People probably do this all the time they just haven't told you about it. Then again many people have never had this experience because such sounds are lost in the hub-

bub of modern life. Naturally they would find it hard to believe in voices different from their own." In the quiet woods
I was listening to sounds others could not hear, the sound of
continuity, the sound of a living earth from which I once
came and to which I still belong. It was a wonderful, wonder-
filled sensation, as if a door had been flung open letting in
the light. It was an awareness, a connection, a beginning.
Krishnamurti wrote, "You have more and more beginnings,
what you never have are endings."

AND A YEAR LATER there was another happening, an or-
dinary occurence, but one which clearly illustrated for me
the importance of several survival patterns in life which I
had not yet fully comprehended. One balmy spring morning
in Maine as I sauntered, camera in hand, along the shore of
the pond I came upon two of nature's many finely timed
cycles: an insect hatch and the arrival of spring birds. Hundreds of dragonfly nymphs emerging from their watery "first
life" were scurrying across the gravelly shore toward the safety
of whatever plant growth they could find while hungry mi-
grant spotted sandpipers bobbed wildly about feasting on this
bounty. The nymphs programed for transformation had no
time to waste, the birds weary from the flight had need of
food. Those who escaped being eaten crawled up and clung

to the first grass or reed they came to. I watched one closely. It hung motionless for what seemed no more than a minute before the nymph suddenly ceased to exist. The shell split open at the neck as the round-eyed head of the dragonfly arched sharply backwards pulling and pulling until the compressed wings popped free of their casing. Very gradually, still poised on the reed, the body straightened, the gossamer wings unfolded and the veins became firm. Then, in a flash it was gone, now a hunter and one of nature's fastest fliers.

On a hot summer's day sitting on the grass outside my cabin I watched a big blue dragonfly cruising just behind and above a large white-faced hornet. In the blink of an eye it attacked snapping the hornet's head off vanishing with the body. The hunter and the flier—an ancient ritual of life governed by silent signals bound to the cycles of earth. As a creature of earth do I have signals deep within? I cannot fly, my talent is to contemplate the flight. But I wonder too if I might have gossamer wings already in place waiting to unfold—twin talents of insight and intuition. Perhaps the ultimate goal for any human is to learn to utilize these gifts, to move with the steady flow of change creating new directions for human flight on the wings of the mind. A voice reminds me that in every spring there is growing to be done and hab-

its to be shed and changes to be made. When wonder illumi-
nates the inner eye, patterns of life become one of many fascinating mysteries.

ON an OLD ROAD to a NEW PLACE

> "And the world cannot be discovered by a journey of miles, no matter how long, but only by a spiritual journey of one inch, very arduous and humbling and joyful, by which we arrive at the ground at our feet, and learn to be at home."
> —Wendell Berry, *The Earth Speaks* (edited by Steve Van Matre)

Change is an unalterable force in life that we must all accept. But the tempo is set by the seasons of each person's life and by the time my husband and I had reached our "middle years" we found it very acceptable to be involved with living at a slower pace. The years of hurried days and busy family life had passed. Our children had grown up and were off on their own. The weeks of summer were no longer bustling with gatherings of young people and we reluctantly sold our beloved Maine cabin with its wide fields and woodlands. Like the farm of my childhood, the country home of my children's youth was no more. I still miss both of them—a measure of my depth of belonging. Each loss had stood as a stark reminder of the passage of time and of life's mandate for change. Any change, chosen or not, is a burden to the spirit because our sense of continuity is being shaken, threatening our inner basic need to belong. When connections are lost and old patterns must be reworked with new ones, it is time to seek silence and listen to the heart, to fulfill old dreams, to open doors and to gradually venture in new directions. And this is most easily begun with old friends in favorite places.

SINCE WE HAD more time to ourselves Ted and I began returning each year during late May to visit the Greenville area and some of the small lakes and camps northeast of Moosehead. While Ted was flyfishing I would explore the woods and nearby wetlands. The more I explored the longer I wanted to stay but soon realized that, if I were to wander alone, I needed a base camp near more easily accessible woodlands and bogs. We tried a number of different places before friends told us about the Bradford Camps on Munsungan Lake, an area unfamiliar to both of us, located well north of Maine's beautiful Baxter State Park. At that time the camp was accessible only by plane so we arranged with Folsom's Flying Service in Greenville to fly us in for a short visit. Dick

Folsom was a Greenville boy who had returned from WWII to his seaplane service (now run by his son Max) on the shore of Moosehead Lake, and I hadn't seen him for years. He had become famous for creating an incredible DC3 seaplane. I saw it once. It roared across the bay as he took it up and then loomed over the town like some great hulking spirit as it came in to land again on the lake— an amazing sight! He laughed when I reminded him of the days when we were young and all crazy to be like "Lindy" and Dick Folsom, a real pilot, was looked upon with awe. And now here I was in the cockpit beside him as excited as I would have been thirty years earlier. This was a special treat for me. He pointed out from the air places I had known as a young person and even circled the area of Baxter Park near Mt. Katahdin, which I had climbed many times. Seeing the north woods as a great expanse of green forest stretching all the way to the horizon moved me deeply. On trips in following years looking down over the same forest lands sliced into pieces by lumber roads bordering huge acreages of cutland was heartbreaking. I felt ashamed for the greed of my own species. But this was my first flight and I saw a seemingly endless green earth flecked with glistening clear waters in all sizes and shapes. It was wonderful. As we approached Munsungan Lake I already knew that this was the country I wanted to see, to roam, to touch and to know. Have you ever had the feeling that there is something special about a place? That perhaps you have been there before or that you belong there but you don't know why? That is how I felt when I arrived at Bradford Camps. Here were woods to wander, brooks to follow, wetlands to explore. We were guests for only a few days but we arranged to return early the next spring. And this land kept drawing me back until I began to stay weeks at a time and even then I wished I could stay forever. When I was in camp I ate breakfast and dinner in the main lodge spending the rest of the time pretty much on my own. These were some of the most exciting weeks in my life in regard to my personal and spiritual growth. During long hours of solitude I became better acquainted with myself listening to the voices in my life which I had been too busy to hear. In the midst of many differently living things I became part of a greater living force. This whole place "spoke to me."

In this north country the old logging roads are overgrown and unused except perhaps during hunting season. They meander through the cutlands criss-crossing and petering out into undergrowth. These dead-end roads presented me with a wonderfully open-ended opportunity: the freedom to go nowhere. In the confines of family living I have not often had that option. I remember the times while raising my family of four children when I would yearn to be free of interruptions and obligations, when I longed for solitude. Some people are uncomfortable without a busy agenda, I am not one of them. In fact I believe I have survived well because occasionally I was fortunate enough to be able to exist away from the artificial routines of modern life, living in a place where I was free to rise with the sun or the moon, free to rest when my body requested it, free to ignore time and let a moment linger for an hour, free to measure the day/night as a series of ongoing scenes. At Bradford Camps I had all of this, plus a place to wander alone and uncommitted in a setting to stimulate the mind or challenge the spirit, whichever seemed to suit my mood.

SOME DAYS I JUST want to hear what the world around me is saying. No searching for flowers, no photography busyness, no marking new trails. Often I have heard people use the phrase, "Get off my back!" and here the thought of it brings me new meaning. As I prepare to lighten my packbasket I realize I have a mental packbasket which I must also lighten. A message seems clear: Bear no burdens and the spirit will open. To set my mind free of intent, I begin with the very clear directive, "Start out!" This is followed by my personal guarantee that I will always get where I am going because "where" will never be decided until I have returned. Sometimes it is days before I discover the "where" that I have been to. This kind of freedom requires that I seek the meaning and the value of the day apart from any preconceived expectations. I become the artist blending the colors on the palette, interpreting the aura of the day. This approach is powerful because I am aware that it involves me in my own creation. The listening and learning and connecting are not easy talents to develop. I try to practice each one when I am wandering alone.

LIGHT OF BURDEN and spirit—one of those kinds of days— I wander early in the morning hours. At first I always feel like HURRYING! Hurrying is a "Glad to be out" way of greeting a day of exploration. Then I slow my gait to fit the quiet of the setting. I walk along the mossy edges of the road to hush my footsteps. It is spring and the forest is alive. The winter wren and the ruby-crowned kinglet merry the woods with their songs. In one sense I have lots of company, in another I am alone—there is no one to talk to. Habit tells me to call out, "Hi! Is anybody home?" Our religious faiths teach us that we are never alone and I believe that; but in our daily lives we are seldom alone long enough to become familiar with alternate means of communication. And that is precisely why it is important to *be alone*, all sole alone and ready to experience a wholeness of being. It cannot be found in a crowd of ideas or people.

On one of my many walks this experience came to me as a gift—I cannot describe it any other way. I did not go in search of it. It was a happening. How or why I am not certain but it came wrapped in a glowing sense of wonder. Perhaps I was so free of boundaries that all my senses created a charged field of awareness or perhaps I was simply ready to receive whatever came my way.

I HAD BEEN walking an hour when I came to a dilapidated log bridge over a brook swollen by spring run-off. Flooding waters had lodged fallen trees and tangled roots  among the boulders on both sides of the stream. I lay down with my chin over the edge of one of the logs watching the cold water roll over the smoothed rocks. Bubbles swirled around the top of a deep pool. I thought of what Alan Ereira had written about the Kogi tribe in the mountains of Columbia. They believed that "communing with water provides access to the memory and the potential of the universe." I wondered what the rushing waters knew of the thundering gorge they were fast approaching. Possibly as much as I have known of the gorges in my own life.

Getting up slowly so as to be kind to my joints I began walking again at an even pace down the center of the road. I could feel the stones under my boots and hear the sound of my footsteps. Thoughts drifted through my mind: "no one knows I have taken this road; no hour has been set for my return. I may walk for however long I wish one step after another there and back wherever 'there' may be. No one waits 'there' to greet me; no gracious hostess will fret because I fail to show; my arrival ceases to exist." The aloneness spreads through me. The road seemed to have become my own, unknown and endless, life and spirit moving together. Absorbed in a reverie I walked an inner road as well.

My boots scuffed against the gravel surface like brushes on a snare drum beating a subtle rhythm:

      scuff, step   scuff, step

        scuff, scuff step, step

until the sound possessed my mind and pulsed through my brain over and over and over. With the hypnotic power of drums and chants the sound rang through my body isolating me from all other sounds, forcing my mind to focus on a pin-point center.

I stopped and stood absolutely still letting the sound of my footsteps fade slowly through my body into an inner core of silence. The moment was entirely peaceful as an aware-ness of my connections to some vital life source flashed through me.

Perhaps I had what Maslow called "a peak experience," an intuitive knowing which many visionaries believe opens us to the fulfillment of human potential, a resource we all have waiting to be tapped. I have read that in Islam the rhythm of walking is used as a technique for dissolving the attachments of the world—a way of losing oneself in God. I felt as if I had swallowed a wholeness pill. Beginnings and endings, joys and sorrows, self and others mingled and blended with spirit. For whatever reason this happened I knew that nothing in my life would appear again as it had before that moment. I felt wide open all the way into the source of my spirit so that I viewed the world through inner eyes tran-scending the limits of self. From that time on this sense of wholeness influenced in varying degrees all my confronta-tions with and contemplations about life. Whitehead spoke of poets whose insights come from "the brooding presence of the whole." Once found such gifts are never truly lost.

DEALING with the NATURAL WORLD

Alaskan eskimo belief: The soul of the universe is never seen. Its voice, however, may be heard on occasion, through innocent children. Or in storms. Or in sunshine. It whispers, "Be not afraid of the universe."

I have often heard the comment that Maine has only two seasons, August and winter. Any mention of spring is avoided. I have always loved spring for the smell of earth, the tenderness of soft greens, the sounds of living. But dispite all the wonderful feelings of release from the confinements of ice and snow spring in Maine does take some getting used to. It is "mud time" when the ground thaws to mush and the roads heave and it is "ice-out" when the streams rush with frigid waters and great rafts of ice, and then, it is "blackfly time." There are reasons for not wishing to prolong a discussion of spring in Maine, and most of them have to do with the hatching of blackflies, every blasted thirty or forty different kinds of them. Just about the time forest animals are beginning to shed their winter layers and fishermen are swarming to buy the newest "sure-fire" lures, insects eager for a blood meal begin to stir. Then, as all of us mammals bask in the first real warmth of the sun the inevitable plague of spring in the north country appears. The blackflies attack—actually blackflies in the daytime, mosquitoes and no-see-ums at night. They say that blackflies and mosquitoes can drive a person crazy. I'll buy that!

During the years when my cameras and I were insepa-rable I was always having a run-in with one insect or an-other. When my friend Dotsy Long, a gifted photographer, introduced me to the wild orchids of New England we spent many hours slogging through wet buggy terrain in pursuit of the flowers of these unusual plants, practically inviting the local bug population to feed on us.

Except for the lady's slipper, which is a common flower in our Massachusetts woodlands I had never seen any or-chids in the wild before in my life. For me they represented a whole new aspect of the north woods. Birds had been my passion for years. Now I went mad for orchids and the bogs where many of them grew. Not rare ones, just easy to over-look or difficult to reach in their specific habitat. Of course, anyone can see these plants by taking guided tours through protected bogs and wetlands of the northeast and Canada but I wanted to see if I could find some of them in my own corner of the woods, and that, in a limited way, is what I set out to do. Humid weather didn't dampen my enthusiasm for being afield in June but the blackflies turned out to be quite another matter. I soon discovered I had an unusual life-threatening allergy to the bite of one (or all) of this species so my plans went on hold while I spent three years being treated by a specialist before I could safely return to any blackfly habitat. I have been most fortunate and when others complain about blackfly bites I urge them to use some sort of available protection. Every year a new product hints at a miracle but from my experience I would say, "Use whatever seems to work best, even if it means just waiting for a cool, windy day when the flies lie low."

It is popular these days to use Avon's Skin-So-Soft as a repellent. I have never tried it but the fragrance is delightful. It tickles my funnybone when I smell it around the macho setting of a fishing camp where some of the guides and even the old hands use it. A nice change, however, from earlier times. Thoreau carried a mixture of oil of turpentine, spearmint and camphor and commented, "The remedy was worse than the disease." I have been told that Indians covered themselves with muddy clay when they had to, but most had the good sense to migrate out of the area during June, which is more than I can say for myself. I go north, eager to greet the spring but when I venture forth I wear a turtleneck, wool kneesocks, long pants, bug jacket and headnet, every piece saturated with repellent. Whether it is ninety degrees or freezing (although I do remove the netting if it is cold) I am covered. And you can smell me coming! No bear in his right mind would care to approach me. Blackflies never hesitated.

The first few years following my allergy treatments Ted and I took brief trips to Maine in May or early June as I tested the effectiveness of the shots. I would set forth out of camp in the morning dressed in my bug-defying outfit, my knapsack on my back, ready to explore places I could reach on foot or in a canoe. Sometimes Ted would leave me off on the far shore of the lake for a few hours while he went fishing.

Hunting for wildflowers is not an adventure which can be hurried, it is an adventure which unfolds. The ambiance of woodland settings needs to be gradually absorbed and enjoyed as one would enjoy a piece of music when its especially beautiful harmonies inspire the soul. I have found that every day brings discoveries, which some might consider insignificant or "old hat." Fine, it is all a matter of attitude. I tend to celebrate whatever it is I find, some things more loudly than others. One of the biggest thrills I have ever had was finding an early spring calypso orchid in a place where none had been recorded before (only because no one had bothered to look). I had found a hidden treasure!

While Ted fished a small trout pond several miles from camp I tramped back and forth in a cedar bog which bordered the northern edge of the pond. Back and forth, back and forth in the deep shade picking my way slowly over the mossy green carpet when suddenly THERE IT WAS! A speck of pink in a sea of green, the tiny "fairy orchid." This one was amazingly small, barely three-quarters of an inch on a delicate stem. I could hardly believe my eyes. Is it brand new, one of many to come and am I the first creature to see it? Or is this one of ancient lineage? Oh, you can see much larger ones in Michigan, Canada or Vermont for that matter, but this one was in *my* Maine woods and I literally danced around shouting, "I found it! I found it!" My dear husband thought something had happened to me and almost fell from his canoe trying to come to my aid. Well, something *had* happened to me and it was wonderful. Later I showed my treasure to a forest ranger who told me that in all his years of walking lines he had never seen one. "I must have gone by them a hundred times. I can't believe it."

Two years later because I was spending longer periods of time at Bradford Camps I had covered most of the wetlands I could reach by myself and decided to hire a guide who could take me by truck or canoe to locations from which we might reach other remote bogs. I could not have known then that because of this decision I would find another real treasure, one Toby Montgomery. This young University of Maine graduate temporarily risked his good reputation as a registered hunting and fishing guide to take a lady old enough to be his grandmother on some crazy posey hunt. He, I am sure, took a ribbing from the other guides (who wouldn't have been caught dead taking me out) while I worried that I might not be able to keep up. I needn't have. One time as we returned from a day of hiking, he told the others, in his kindly way, "She wore me out!"—a delightful exaggeration. Together Toby and I have found twenty species of orchids (the latest being the lovely yellow lady's slipper hidden in the soft greens of the cedars). And there were many more we could have found if we had been free to devote two weeks out of every month from May to October tramping the land. But no matter, every find was a delight and every search an adventure—one became almost too thrilling, certainly not a typical orchid hunt.

AFTER ENDURING a day or two of blackflies most people begin to pray for wind and rain to bring a reprieve from the torment. And their prayers are apt to be answered because storms, brief and furious, also breed in steamy hot weather. In this north country you had best understand the warning signs for these storms—your life may depend upon it. The power in a speeding storm front is awesome to behold and when several swirl together they are frightening to endure. Anyone who has been in the wild has experienced a major storm at least once. Weather like this is difficult to read and can be impossible to avoid. I will vouch for the authenticity of that remark.

Early in the morning of an oppressively hot June day I climbed into a truck loaded with a canoe and assorted para-phernalia ready to go off on an "orchid treasure hunt" with Toby. Neither of us could have had any idea as we embarked on our first canoe trip together that it would be one we would never forget: not the kind you can prepare for, the kind you simply face.

We were headed for a lake about thirty miles away to the north of camp which Toby knew had a wide bog at its eastern end. As we bounced and lurched along the road I began enthusiastically describing the orchids I hoped we might find on the bog, flowers he had heard of but never seen. Road is a term used loosely here to mean both the main crushed stone guaranteed-to-slash-tires highway, domain of the huge lumber trucks, and the endless miles of old logging roads winding over ledges and through brushy swales. We rattled over the rough roads passing only a few fine stands of trees among the acres and acres of cutland and slash before we came over a ridge shorn of its forest where we caught our first glimpse of the lake. Near the bottom of the hill Toby turned right, drove a short distance parallel to the shore and parked in an abandoned loading station shaded by overarching white birches, hardwood trees left when the soft-woods were harvested.

Toby portaged the canoe to the edge of the lake and loaded our camera bags and packs. We were on the south side of a broad cove ringed by a band of tall evergreens mock-ingly called "the beauty strip," a buffer required of the lum-ber companies around bodies of water. In the shade beneath these trees clusters of pure white lady's slippers flowered. The less familiar name of moccasin flower seemed more appropriate to this setting. I have found that in this area they are usually white while the ones near my Massachusetts home are almost always rosy pink. As we took up our paddles ospreys began calling overhead and two bald eagles checked the lake. They will steal an osprey's catch of fish if they get the chance. Rounding the point of the cove gave us our first view of the sweep of the lake. To our left and at a slight angle from us I could see the grassy stretch of bog growth which covered most of the eastern end of the lake. Early spring bird calls came from every direction. The clear peeping calls of nesting spotted sandpipers confirmed their presence on the two rock islands which lay between us and the bog where a snipe was holding forth. The male does "hold forth" too. He pipes brassy calls from a stump or dead treetop, then flings himself into a crazy twirling zigzag flight intended to attract a mate. Watching these antics I told Toby about one of my friends who named the resident snipe on his farmland "Fruitcake." When we reached the bog we poked along the edge, got out, checked briefly then moved on until we came to the north edge where a nice stream emptied out of the lake. Toby tied the canoe there and we both began hunting in earnest. He came up the winner, his first too. "I think I have found one. It' pink!" he shouted. I came running—well, not really, you can't run on a quaking surface. I don't know which of us was more excited.

There it was—a small arethusa barely six inches high with its flower, the Dragon's mouth, almost lost in the remains of dried grasses. Further south in New England I had seen larger and more vivid ones growing in their primitive bog setting. But when I saw those there was none of the excitement of finding this in its cold north country tableau where it is apt to be miniature in size and pale in color. Searching further we eventually found other arethusa, swamp rose, violets, plants of all kinds. The whole place was a wonderland to explore.

As the morning passed the air became heavy and still— so still that it alerted us. We kept looking to the north and west at the ring of high ridges beyound the open expanse of the lake for any sign of lurking storms. We were vulnerable and we knew it. Distant thunder rumbled closer. Then suddenly with the motion of a huge dark hunched-back monster a storm bounded over the ridges and across the water directly at us. Toby raced to pull the canoe up turn it over and anchor it on the bog. We scrambled into rain gear, stuffed our camera bags under the canoe and made for the only bit of cover anywhere around, two stubby tamaracks. Plunked on stiff twigs of the Labrador-tea (a common shrub in bogs) with our backs against the little trees we curled up over our knees in tight balls as the storm hit. My hood buried me in the dark. The wild wind reminded me of a blizzard I had once been in, only this time the roar was mixed with the sound of torrents of water and the ear-splitting thunder of jagged lightning and the strange smell of ionized air. Then as I listened the sound of the lake changed dramatically. Instead of splashing waves it became a heavy plopping sound. Keeping low I twisted around until I could see beyond the edge of the bog. The whitecaps churned by the wind had disappeared as if a thick oil had quieted the surface—the kind of thing sailors do to temporarily calm the sea in an emergency. Everywhere plumes of water spurted upwards as if propelled by airjets from beneath the surface sending smooth circular ripples out from the center. It was the strangest sight. I thought hail might be hitting the water but we were only a few yards away and none was hitting us. I had noticed a similiar pattern when hard rain fell straight down on water but never like this. Had electrical charges gathered the moisture into huge high speed raindrops? The next second the whitecaps returned and more drenching rain. I was soaked to the skin. New fabrics may be popular but they aren't much good in a "real rain." I thought longingly of the oilskin slicker and Gloucester fisherman's hat I wore as a child. And then I got hungry. Thinking our food, Toby's many sandwiches and my saltines, were nearby under the canoe I suggested lunch. "Might as well eat, we're stuck for awhile."

"Well," Toby slowly strung out his response, "I wouldn't want you telling people that I served you soggy crackers (pause) so I left them in the truck."

"What! You didn't!" I burst into laughter—better than food it was the touch of humor we needed just about then.

Storms from different directions continued to roll and tangle together surrounding us with dark ominous clouds and flashing light and thunder. We never moved—hungry or not food could wait. After an hour or so there was a letup in the rain as some of the storms passed to the south of us. We quickly loaded the canoe and started paddling back along the edge of the bog in the direction we had come. Twice brilliant spears of lightning forced us to abandon the canoe and flatten ourselves against the soggy sphagnum mat. Another hour passed. We discussed the situation, studied the cloud patterns, counted the pauses between flash and thunder and weighed the risks . If necessary we could bushwhack around the shore of the lake to our starting place, but tall trees can he a hazard in weather like this. (Later, we found out how hazardous). We knew we could be in as much danger on the shore as on the lake so we waited, chose a moment and committed ourselves to the trip across open water. One hundred yards out with no warning lightning struck nearby. I leaned as low as I could and paddled! My thoughts were as wild as the wind: If we are hit will the canoe split? Where are the keys to the truck? I don't even know the way back to camp. Could I save Toby if he were stunned? Flicks on fast forward! I never paddled so fast nor so hard in my life. I never looked up, just trusting Toby to steer the course. When we reached shore we both laughed with relief and shook our heads—WOW! Back beside the truck we discovered that one of the high birches had been splintered by lightning indicating that danger from this storm had few limits. Then as we started on the road we came upon unbelievable destruction. On the south side of one ridge for as far as we could see on both sides of the road every one of the trees in this stand I admired in the morning had been torn up by the roots. In other places trees lay helter-skelter in twisted chaos. It was shocking to see. But we were lucky because loggers, woodsmen, guides and camp owners go into high gear when something like this happens and they all go out to help. By the time we came along someone had already cut openings around the larger trees which had fallen across the road and Toby managed to clear or skirt around smaller ones. Finally back in camp warm, dry and well fed we listened to other stories about the storms of the day. For a young man the likes of Toby our day presented a lively adventure; for me, it was one to contemplate. There had been the threat of extreme danger but that had not seemed to matter. I had only been acutely aware of the intensity of living. It was as if I could feel the life force propelling me into the future, creating my newest past from my immediate present, making out of all those fleeting moments one pulse of time, my whole life in one flowing beat.

MEETINGS with FELLOW TRAVELERS

"My own true inner being actually exists in every creature ..." —Joseph Campbell, *The Inner Reaches of Outer Space*

O ver the years I have noticed that after I have lectured about my various wanderings the questions I am asked most concern being alone. The idea of my walking by myself in the north woods alarms people. Even while I was staying at Munsungan Lake a young couple, the Kamps from Connecticut, checked to be sure I had a compass and even gave me a small one to pin on my shirt. They returned the next year and when I arrived for supper after being on one of my day's adventures they announced to everyone present: "Our friends in Connecticut thought we were really strange to go so far away *just to fish*. So we said, If you think *we* are strange, wait 'til we tell you about this lady we met who hikes around bogs all day *by herself*!" I have wondered whether it is the woods or being alone that makes people feel uncomfortable. Are we so accustomed to crowds and noise and entertainment that we no longer know how to handle being alone? How to amuse ourselves? How to perceive aloneness as a creative interlude for personal growth? One young family had decided I must have had a dog with me and were amazed when I told them I did not. "Aren't you afraid? What if you fall? Meet a wild animal? Get lost?"

I like to think of myself as cautious and well prepared for emergencies: my L.L.Bean packbasket contained twenty pounds of camera equipment plus an endless list of everything from field guides and topo maps to Swiss army knife and a whistle. I was prepared for everything—except my emotions. When I discovered one day that I was totally lost, off the trail as usual and in a new area, all I wanted to do was yell: "Somebody get me out of this place!" Fine Indian I would have made. I'll bet Indians never screamed. Never got lost either. I suppose I could be forgiven. I was a beginner in my fifties and the forest was not my home. After my initial wave of panic subsided I examined the topos, chose my direction and tramped through slash and swamp until I came upon the remnants of a road I could identify on the map. So I wasn't really lost. I just didn't know where I was for a few hours: no different from when life's scene of action has left me feeling lost for a time. I learned. Later whenever I ventured into unfamiliar territory I tied pieces of surveyor's tape to branches, carefully removing them as I returned so as not to clutter the woods.

Was I afraid? Afraid of meeting wild animals? No, and certainly not of being alone. Maybe I will be sometime but I am usually too busy thinking about what I might find next. People mistakenly think of me as living *with* the animals like the research professionals who record their amazing relationships with wild creatures for television nature programs. Oh, I have seen bear, fisher, deer, moose, fox, coyote, beaver and all sorts of birds and little creatures but most animals I see run for cover, thus any close encounters have been a surprise to us both. Some became humorous in the telling, some filled me with awe, none was dangerous. Danger is driving on the highway where 37,000 deaths occur each year. In our western parks black bears that have learned to scavenge for food at dumps and campsites are a serious problem and we are beginning to have the same problem in the east but not for me. I stay in a cabin, carry only dried snacks and place my pack at a distance from me when I take it off. In early spring bears roam hundreds of acres foraging for wild food and often wander into camp so there are frequent signs of their presence and some sightings but they don't stay long. One swam across the lake in broad daylight but I was on a hike and missed the show. Another time at the brook behind the main lodge Ted and I came upon a handsome bruin, glossy black and huge, who disappeared in a flash. Hard to believe how fast such a large animal could travel through thick woods. That was as close as I ever got to a bear although I once slept outside at the edge of the lake hoping to take a picture by moonlight of one which was hanging around camp. I spent two miserable nights in cold air and heavy dew with only pictures of the moon and a good story to show for it. Actually for all my talk if a bear should ever confront me I think I would snap a few pictures and faint. So much for bravery.

TV specials and movies make it look easy to confront wild animals. It is not. However, if you are overcome by the desire to experience such closeness may I suggest that it is easier to stay calm and it can be just as inspiring as being on safari, perhaps more so, if you first try to approach a benign creature such as a small bird or a frog or a toad. I was on the ground once in a grove of fir trees photographing the tiny white blossoms of gold thread when a toad joined me. Since I was lying flat out on his territory I guess I should say that I joined him. From six inches away his golden eyes studied my blue ones. Then, evidently satisfied with my being there, he draped one leg over a broken twig and watched as if indeed I did belong in his world. Such a wonderful feeling of acceptance! One of those spirit to spirit moments when I could sense the reality of deeper connections, the kind of moment which must be experienced because it can never be captured on film.

Large animals do not usually allow humans to approach them in the wild except on professionally planned trips so I had never seriously entertained the idea of getting close to one. But I never forgot a film I had seen on television which recorded an unusual encounter with orcas (killer whales). Researchers were recording the voices of the whales migrating along the Alaskan coast. From a small boat circling one of the bays a young man in a wet suit slipped into the water carrying a violin and bow held in his hands above his head. As he drifted along in the water he began to play notes which mimicked the songs of the orcas. A pod of whales appeared calling and cavorting around him, their huge heads rising a few feet from his face in what seemed like a celebration. It was a poignant scene of recognition between species. Since then I had fostered the hope that I might someday experience that knowing. And then, quite by surprise, it happened.

It was a beautiful May morning in northern Maine and

I was excited about being in a new place, a sheltered bog at the east end of a small lake. The rhodora was covered with bright pink blossoms while the Labrador tea was in tight bud with barely a hint of white, but I was interested only in photographing the carnivorous sundew and pitcher plants that grew beneath these shrubs in the tangled squashy mat of spaghnum mosses. Moose were abundant in the area and their well worn trails threaded through the bog in every direction. Travel was easy for them on the open bog and being excellent swimmers offered them quick access to both water and forest. Before I ventured out alone I questioned a guide about safety, "You won't have any trouble this time of year. Just don't get between the moose and its escape route," he said, neglecting to tell me how to determine which route the moose would be likely to favor. Basically it is a matter of knowing the creature's habits and doing whatever seems acceptable, as humans do when they visit a different culture. As I walked out onto the bog all I knew about moose was that they were BIG and defended with their front hooves.

Setting my packbasket on a hillock of grass I roamed around on the moose trails until I located a nice patch of both sundew and pitcher plants handy to the edge of a trail. I marked the spot with my hat and went back to collect my stuff. Leaving the basket where it was I hung one camera from my neck, took the tripod in one hand and the close-up camera in the other and returned to my hat where I proceeded to stretch out along the trail. The tripod kept one camera dry while I used the other.

Cool water gradually soaked the front of me as a warming sun blanketed my back - a lovely contrast. I lay perfectly still, a giant scrutinizing a land of Lilliputians. Through the close-up lens of the camera I could see every glandular hair on the fringe of the sundew leaves, tiny rose-colored fans adorned with a diadem of sparkling droplets. Their fancy costume masks their true intent: to trap and feed upon the unwary of their world. A blackfly comes too close: "Good catch!" say I, "Sundew, I wish you a million more." Insect traps are plentiful in the understory of the bog. The pitcher plant is gorgeous and deadly too, with pitcher shaped leaves each holding a quiet pool of water which lures the insect to the edge. Are they attracted by the water or by its reflection? In either case how easily we can be misled by ornate displays.

While contemplating my latest insights I heard a noise behind and to my left nearer the water's edge. No, I *felt* the noise vibrate ever so gently through me. So, I straightened up to look around. There, coming toward me on *her* path, was a cow moose! Now, a cow moose may not be large compared to the bull with a full rack but compared to 120 pounds of five and a half foot Waldron, her 500 pounds of six-foot moose ranked high. I immediately set my close-up camera in my hat on the moss, stood up with the other camera dangling from my neck, grabbed the tripod for moral support and said (politely I thought), "Go away!" This only served to arouse her curiosity, she was more like me than I had realized. She kept coming, eyes on me every second. At the junction of her trail and the one I was on she turned directly toward me. There I stood, double the height of any bush in the whole bog, glaringly out of place, trying to decide whether this moose preferred an escape route through water or woods, both of which seemed readily available to her. She continued in my direction. Obviously escape was not her intent.

We were both bedraggled. I was dripping wet and wore around my neck a grungy kerchief which reeked of repellent. She was shedding her winter coat in shaggy pieces which left her a motley brown, but her eyes were beautiful. Finally I dropped the tripod and began snapping pictures in rhythm with her steps: click, approach (hers), "Go away" (mine); click, approach, "Go away." Seven frames later she stopped less than a yard from me, lowered her head to my level and stared. No laid-back ears, no threatening move. I was struck by her clear eyes and quiet breathing. Loren Eiseley wrote, "One does not meet oneself until one catches the reflection

from an eye other than human." I wish now I had reached out to pat her long face. Moments passed, which seemed endless at the time. Then she turned away, slipped gracefully into the water and swam off. I felt dismissed. Creature to creature I found her beautiful. It was enough.

LESSONS from NEW PLACES

"I wonder if there are not memories within our genes that the conscious mind has not yet learned to tap, memories of experience as well as those of form and character. How else explain the inner stirrings that come from close contact with the earth?"
Charles Lindberg, *Feel the Earth* (Reader's Digest, 1972)

Several years ago while I was staying at Bradford Camps, Dave Youland invited me to fly with him to a remote pond where he owned a camp he was preparing for rental. After an early supper we took off flying north high above the rugged land. The green forest seemed to ripple endlessly toward the horizon and hundreds of small lakes and ponds popped into view as we passed over the ridges which hid them. A half hour later as the plane rose over a peak Dave banked sharply to come in on a tiny pond. I could look down into clear deep water held in a forest-green bowl. We landed, tied the plane to a makeshift dock and walked up to a little cabin perched like a falcon's eyrie on a ledge. In a matter of minutes Dave had checked everything and we were once again airborne. The winds had died down completely and from above all the lakes and ponds had become mirrors reflecting the glowing evening colors. In every direction rose and white whisps of clouds floated in silvery peach liquid as if pieces of the sunset had been scattered about upon the landscape in a glorious surrealistic display.

ALTHOUGH I HAD seen the place only briefly, during the following winter I felt "a calling," a deep need to be there by myself. Since Ted was planning a late May fishing trip with our son I chose the same week for my sojourn alone. On the morning of May 31, 1988 a brisk northwest wind was blowing fat puffy clouds across the sky. Dave loaded my sleeping bag, packbasket with knapsack, camera, clothes, paddle and food and (prophetically) a copy of John Hanson Mitchell's *Ceremonial Time* into his Supercub and I climbed aboard laughing and waving to husband and son as we took off. My whole body was excited. I could have flown under my own power, just stretched out my wings and soared! By the time we had arrived at the pond a strong wind had come up which made the landing difficult and could make it impossible for the plane to clear the ridge at take-off so we hurried to unload. Then as soon as Dave had opened the cabin, pointed out where necessaries like ax, matches, bucket, life jacket and canoe were stashed he departed, telling me he would return in five days, weather permitting. I climbed the hill to the little cabin and sat on the steps wondering why I had been called to come alone, yet feeling as if I had been waiting all my life to be in this spot.

Through spindly thin spruce trees I could see the pond spread in a circle before me. Moose were feeding in a wide cedar bog to my left. On the far shore to my right an open wetland and a brook bordered a deep cove. I would have liked

to explore that one in the canoe but the wind was blowing in strong gusts, so that would have to wait. Instead I spent the day wandering the surrounding woods. First, however, I unrolled my sleeping bag , stuffed my clothing inside where it would stay dry and warm and also serve as a pillow, hung raingear and camera bag on nails along the wall, and shoved my everyday fully equiped knapsack under the bed freeing up my packbasket for further duty as a kindling carrier. I have always had "a thing" about my supply of kindling, sort of a be-prepared-and-comfy syndrome from my wood stove days with my children. No fire was started until kindling for the next day was on hand. Now as I looked for flowers I filled the basket with sticks and branches to store under the cabin for a rainy day. A few white lady's slippers were in bloom, lots of twinflower and bunchberry covered the ground and clintonia were in bud but I saw no sign of any trillium, which was a disappointment. Finally, knowing I had chores to do before dark I headed back to the cabin. By the time I had hauled water up the steep ledge from the pond, mended the one available screen, eaten supper and stacked wood inside for the morning fire, the sun had set. I waited outside for the first star to appear before I closed the door against the cool night air. Dressed in long winters and a warm shirt I stretched out on my sleeping bag content to dissolve into the setting.

Hours later I was awakened by something. I got up to open the door. My world was floodlit by a full moon—a very special one I later discovered, a Blue Moon, the second full moon of the month. Had moonbeams tapped at my door? I pulled on boots and a windbreaker and went outside.

I sat on the ground in front of the cabin with my back against a tree listening. No loons were calling and the night was strangely quiet. Silhouettes of spruce trees framed the path of the moonlight stretching from across the pond to the shore at the foot of the steep drop in front of me. A snowshoe rabbit, perhaps an emissary from the Great Hare who formed the earth, joined me. We waited side by side a yard apart. From a distant ridge I could hear the hoo-hooing of a barred owl, the muted voice of an oracle. Then a breeze or a spirit or another "something" stirred the surface of the water, making it look as if someone were walking directly toward us on the silvery path. I was spellbound, barely breathing. Suddenly, from somewhere or somehow, I heard the question gently asked,"Who are you?" Into the hushed night I whispered, "I am Wandering White-bird." Where that came from I had

no idea. The sound of my voice never disturbed the rabbit, he didn't move. Time passed or did not exist. Then a gentle wind erased the moonway and the rabbit quietly disappeared. I lingered alone watching the shadows unable to explain this gift of a vision.

The next morning the air was cold and dark gray clouds moved among little patches of blue sky. I was glad for the warmth of the fire in the little wood stove. My arrival yesterday seemed eons ago. The spruce woods, the cabin and the spell of the night had wrapped me in another dimension. As I began reading John's book his stories added to my mood. He mentioned names similiar to the one I had taken last night as mine, but I hadn't heard them before. Had I thought of it because the snowy owl had for years been a kind of totem to me? I had no answer. And where was I last night? I had experienced something which I needed to understand. I read on. John wrote of people who communicate "on the level of thoughts and feelings" and experience "right feelings" for places, as if he were confirming the recent events in my life. Then, as he described how he quietly watched his three Indian friends perform an ancient ritual dance he said, "I felt that I was transported back into some indistinct period in the time before time." I began to realize that now is all of time and our spirits which are connected to all living things at all times may be witness to timeless events. Thinking in this manner brought me amazing peace. This pond, the water, the circling ridge and the sky had called me to discover my spiritual bonds, ties from life's primal connection.

COMFORTABLE WITH this thought I finally fixed myself some breakfast, ate, packed my gear and set out in the canoe for the far shore to explore the wetland area I had noticed when I arrived. The air felt more like October than June. Half way across the pond one of the blacker clouds opened up dumping hail and rain with a *shwoosh*. It was fantastic! I didn't dare stop paddling to put on my raincoat. Hail bounced all around—off the knapsack, cushions and me as I hunkered down in the middle of the canoe and paddled like mad until I was able to reach a cove in the lee of the wind where I grounded the canoe on what appeared to be a well used Moose trail. Ice sparkled everywhere and quickly disappeared. I climbed out, put on a wool hat, down vest and raincoat to capture the warmth I had generated. Thank heaven I was wearing wool kneesocks and heavy wool pants—wet but warm. Wool, don't leave home without it!

Then I looked around me. What a spot! The wetland was indeed a quaking bog covered with bog shrubs and plants of all kinds ready to burst into bloom. It was beautiful and quiet. Birds sang only once during a brief show of sun, too cold for song. After scouting the whole area I started back paddling slowly along the shore, stopping to check a stand of cedars for any sign of the calypso orchid. Staying near shore is interesting, for me anyway. That's where the action is and, should the weather turn bad, I know I can pull the canoe along in the shallows until I eventually circle back to the camp. Small ponds like this one let me feel "at home" on them. I wouldn't want to wander on big lakes or the ocean. I wouldn't have the ties I need.

Bruce Chatwin's book *The Songlines* describes how early Indian tribes along our northwest coast traveled following a songline much like that of the Australian aborigines. The navigator for a trip would be a woman shaman or priestess who created a song, a verbal map, describing the water and the land as they journeyed. When they wished to return she would sing the song in reverse. Once created the song would be preserved by the shamans, the keepers of the tribal history. Recently I read that researchers have translated some of the earliest shaman songs and have been able to identify and locate the places on a modern map. That set me to wondering. If these ancient songs handed down generation to generation are accurate, is the whale's song also a legend of the pod's travels? And, long, long ago did we leave the sea knowing a song? Could I "listen back" far enough to recall it by adjusting my brain waves to the correct frequency? Is that what ESP, other lives, other voices is all about—learning to control the electric energy of our brains? Why not? We put our trust in unbelievable connections every day: cordless phones; TV from around the world picked up and sorted by a "dish" in the backyard; photographs of Jupiter taken by a man in Houston on a camera millions of miles in space; medical treatments using brain waves, sound waves and lasers. No wires, no hocus-pocus just the sending and receiving of signals—the same thing our brain does twenty-four hours a day. If the power center is already there perhaps we also have the connections for hearing our original song—and others. Perhaps humans have many options for communicating beyond time and space.

I wish now I had created a songline every time I had gone exploring alone in a canoe. Backwards or forwards I'd be enjoying my adventures all over again. I have always loved the ambiance of canoeing. It is so very different from a walk in the forest. I take off from land in an open cradle supported by the water and travel into another world. Paddling alone is about as close as one can get to a primal experience. John McPhee calls it "a rite of oneness." Freed of the confinements of land I feel as if I have become a winged spirit moving quietly over the water passing among the tops of mirrored trees and floating with reflected clouds. Every time I return from drifting on the water I have to reattach myself to my land-locked existence.

By the time I got back to camp the sun was dropping behind the ridge and the wind had died down. I unloaded, hauled the canoe up onto shore, turned it over and stashed the paddles(mine and an extra) underneath. Reluctant to leave I put my pack to one side and sat down at the water's edge to watch the evening light fade. Spotted sandpipers scurried among the pebbles on the shore as a female merganser led her parade of nine ducklings bobbing and splashing through the shallows. Further out loons were feeding in golden pools of afterglow. It was a shining scene—shining and completely peaceful, the way I felt. As I stared at the rippling waters they swept every thought from my head. Then, quite suddenly, I no longer saw rippling water. I saw in vivid detail a scene from childhood: It was late winter shortly after my tenth birthday and I was lying in a hospital bed where I had been for several weeks seriously ill with pleurisy. It was painful to breath. My father and two nurses were beside my bed telling me that the little girl my age across the hall had gone home. In the days before miracle drugs patients were carefully isolated so even brief contacts with others acquired special significance, a happy moment in a long day. Ruth was the only patient I ever saw and then only on sunny days when the nurses bundled us up in wool hats and blankets and rolled our beds onto an open porch for a few minutes.

But her mother always waved to me. Now I would be alone and I wanted to go home too.

Suddenly, right then, fifty years after the fact, I heard for the very first time the sounds of that day: crying, whispering and the closing of my door. The picture was complete. Ruth had not "gone home" at all. Ruth had died. My father probably knew that I might never get home, and that the idea of going home to my sisters and brother just might give me an edge on recovery. Going home meant only one thing to me, my father left it at that. The truth had been presented wisely to me in the only shape I could accept at the time. This revelation amazed me. The soft glow of understanding gave the approaching darkness a comfortable feeling. Perhaps after all I was called to this place to learn about myself and last night's vision had simply prepared the way.

DISTANT VOICES

"Beyond the world of the life force is the realm of the spirit."
Tom Brown, *The Quest*

N o sound of spring in the north woods is more eerie at night or more inspiring than the call of the loon rising from the dark waters of a lake. Some legends describe it as the cry of a wounded warrior. At times the sound is so human it almost requires an answer. Thoreau heard the loons often on his trips through northern Maine and felt "as if its [the loon's] language were but a dialect of my own ... awake at night I listened to hear some words or syllables." Cleveland Bent in his monumental *Life Histories of American Birds* refers to a seldom heard peculiar and weird "storm call" which old guides regard as a sure sign of a storm. Bent also mentions that a sweet potato (ocarina) with a D51/2 pitch closely resembles the call. As kids we cupped our hands together and blew through the space between our bent thumbs.

It worked very well with practice. Like most people who are truly familiar with the north country, every time I hear a loon's plaintive call lingering in the night air emotions well up within me as if in response to some deep and mysterious understanding.

When I returned for a second time to stay alone in Dave Youland's remote camp I heard a loon serenade I shall never forget. I had arrived by plane in the morning and had spent the day in the canoe exploring my favorite areas along the brook and wetlands. I had found a loon's nest on the edge of the banking along the far side of the pond. Loons are awkward on land because their legs, which are designed for swimming not walking, are positioned far back in their bodies so they must choose nest sites that enable them to slip easily into the water. There is usually an active pair on this pond and I hoped they were around although I saw no sign of them. But I hadn't checked the nest knowing that if they were nearby my presence might cause them to desert it. By the time I had returned to the cabin and finished the usual chores the wind had shifted into the north and the air was turning cold. I was tired and ready to collapse into my sleeping bag when a loon began calling from somewhere on the pond. So I went outside to sit on the cabin steps. Fingers of night were reaching out from the forest to erase the last light of evening. Another loon answered.

Suddenly as I listened they began a sequence of repetitions which sounded like closely syncopated handbells mimicking one phrase after another. Crescendos affecting the quality of the calls seemed to thrust their cries through the clear night air. My entire being was carried away on the wings of these eerie melodies as the notes circled the pond and skipped through the forest, rising and ringing in one glorious chorus.

Loons had awakened me many times with loud yodeling but this was a combination I had never heard before. Then, in a flash, I realized what was happening. ECHOES! The loons were playing with their echoes! I held my breath it was so awe-inspiring to hear. But how had they learned this amazing technique? Once learned is the gift handed on in their genes to their offspring? Or would any loon know how to use an echo? Later while on a canoe trip my guide Ray Reitze told me that he had heard a similar performance by loons on another small remote lake in a different area of the north woods.

Perhaps this song is sung only on rare occasions and I had been privileged to attend the concert, and may never hear it again. Afterwards I lay in the cabin wondering: would either of these loons, lacking a mate, call in vain to its own echo?

Echoes are the background voices in everyone's life.

Some fade with the kindness of time, some require an answer, some continue to speak. In my own song I can hear repeated harmonies, echoes from every scene along the road I have traveled blending with new echoes created in my immediate present as it sweeps into the past. And I am propelled toward the future, listening for what may yet be, confident that there is much more. Yes, the loons will call again. The song does not end here—it echoes forever, variations on the theme of life.

WALKABOUT

Let me wander in the forest
    Let me tarry on the way
        Let me drift upon the water
        Let me watch the winds at play
    Let me linger in the evening
    Let me tryst with end of day
        Let me gaze up at the heavens
        Let me leave my feet of clay
    Let me catch a timeless vision
    As my spirit breaks away.

Nan Turner Waldron

EPILOGUE

The notes of the flute are the call of the soul.
An Anasazi belief

Last summer I returned for a brief visit to the pond where "my" little cabin stood—but I didn't go by plane and I didn't go alone. Early on a hot July morning Toby took me there by way of land. I soon found out that getting there by truck and on foot required a good deal more effort and energy than flying had but it was a lovely way to approach this place. And, too, I felt comfortable with him because Toby is quiet in the woods and respects the setting. We bumped along on some old wood roads for close to an hour until the road died in front of us. That was it, for wheels anyway. Carrying our paddles, life jackets and packs we hiked down a rocky trail through the moist green woods toward the pond. It was well hidden. Even when we arrived I could barely see the surface of the water through the thick undergrowth of alders along the shore. While I waited Toby went after his stashed canoe. The sun was shining—the air smelled wet—I basked in the silence. Presently, I caught sight of Toby walking in my direction dragging the canoe behind him on the mossy growth under the spruce trees. He loaded our things, pushed the bow into the brushy alders and told me to get in. I ducked down under the branches to reach my seat and he shoved off. As I straightened up, filled with the joy of once again being in this familiar place, the notes of a flute drifted on the air. I quickly turned to look at Toby. Neither of us spoke. Three notes, again, clear and beautiful. "Somebody must be using the cabin," he said. "I'll go over in that direction." I stroked my paddle through the water. The notes rang softly just once more. When we came into the cove where Dave had landed the plane we could see that the cabin was tightly boarded up. No camper, no musician was there. We headed across to the bog where in the past I had spent many hours by myself. The water level was high but we slogged around for about an hour anyway, searching for flowers before we continued to circle the pond. At no time did we see or hear another human being. As we paddled leisurely back toward the trail opening Toby began suggesting ways in which the wind could have made sounds like a flute by blowing through tangled branches or holes in a dead tree. Finally he announced, "There has to be a logical explanation!" I simply turned and smiled at him.

Harmony with the universe must be learned a few notes at a time.

A few suggestions for adventuring with the mind. Any one of these books, which catches your interest, will lead to a dozen more. The choices are endless.

Daniel L. Alkon, M.D, *Memory's Voice*
Herbert Benson, M.D., *Beyond the Relaxation Response*
Daniel B. Botkin, *Discordant Harmonies*
Tom Brown, Jr., *The Quest*
William H. Calvin, *The Cerebral Symphony*
Joseph Campbell, *The Inner Reaches of Outer Space*
Fritjof Capra, *Web of Life*
Bruce Chatwin, *The Songlines*
Loren Eiseley, *The Unexpected Universe*
Alan Ereira, *The Elder Brothers*
Victor E. Frankl, *The Unheard Cry for Meaning*
Shakti Gawain, *Return to the Garden*
Philip Goldberg, *The Intuitive Edge*
G. I. Gurdjieff, *Meetings with Remarkable Men*
Carl A. Hammerschlag, *The Dancing Healers*
Robert Franklin Leslie, *In the Shadow of a Rainbow*
Robert J. Lifton, *The Protean Self and The Broken Connection*

Jerry Mander, *In the Absence of the Sacred*

A. H. Maslow, *The Farther Reaches of Human Nature*

Rollo May, *The Courage to Create and The Cry for
        Myth*

John McPhee, *The Survival of the Bark Canoe*

John Hanson Mitchell, *Ceremonial Time*

Richard Nelson, *The Island Within*

P. D. Ouspensky, *In Search of the Miraculous*

Kenneth Ring, Ph.D., *Life at Death*

Michael J. Roads, *Talking with Nautre*

Carl Sagan, *The Dragons of Eden*

Lyall Watson, *The Lightning Bird*

Brian L. Weiss, M.D., *Many Lives, Many Masters*

ABOUT THE AUTHOR

NAN TURNER WALDRON spent childhood summers on a farm in the north woods of Maine that led to an addition to wild places. She became in adult life an active conservationist, a naturalist and birdwatcher, and a nature photographer. She has been a member of the Appalachian Mountain Club since the 1930s.

For many years she has delivered an annual series of lectures accompanied by slides to various groups throughout New England. In 1974 Nan's work in support of conservation was recognized by Massachusetts Audubon Society with an Audubon Award.

Nan and her husband Ted raised their four children in Sharon, Massachusetts, and now reside in Eastham on Cape Cod. They spend several weeks in the spring and summer in Maine. North Woods Walkabout is Nan's second book.